UNUSUAL Histories

The Electrifying, Action-Packed,

UNUSUAL HISTORY OF Video Games

BY THOMAS JAMES MALTMAN

Content Consultant: Gary Geisler
PhD, Assistant Professor
School of Information
University of Texas at Austin

CAPSTONE PRESS
a capstone imprint

Velocity is published by Capstone Press,
151 Good Counsel Drive, P.O. Box 669, Mankato, Minnesota 56002.
www.capstonepub.com

Printed in the United States of America in Stevens Point, Wisconsin.
032010
005741WZF10

Books published by Capstone Press are manufactured with paper
containing at least 10 percent post-consumer waste.

Library of Congress Cataloging-in-Publication Data
Maltman, Thomas James, 1971–
   The electrifying, action-packed, unusual history of video games / by Thomas
James Maltman.
   p. cm.
   Includes bibliographical references and index.
   Summary: "Describes the history of video games, featuring little known facts and
bizarre inside information"—Provided by publisher.
   ISBN 978-1-4296-4792-2 (library binding)
   1. Video games—History. I. Title.
GV1469.3.M35 2011
794.809—dc22   2010014611

Editorial Credits

Editor: Brenda Haugen
Designer: Veronica Correia
Media Researcher: Wanda Winch
Production Specialist: Eric Manske

Photo Credits

Images Capstone except:
Alamy: Pictorial Press Ltd, 33; Corbis: Ralf-Finn Hestoft, 39 (top), Roger Ressmeyer, 19;
Entertainment Software Rating Board: The ESRB rating icons are registered trademarks of the
Entertainment Software Association, 35 (middle); Getty Images Inc.: AFP/Jeff Christensen,
44, Photographer's Choice/Colin Anderson, cover, SSPL, 25 (top), Tom Munnecke, 24
(top), Time Life Pictures/Walter Sanders, 8-9; Newscom: WENN/Stefan Krempl, 10-11;
Shutterstock: Andrewshka, 36-37 (bkgrnd), Ariel Vaju, 30 (middle), bouzou, 26 (closed sign),
Bruce Rolff 41 (bkgrnd), Catmando, 1, 40 (bkgrnd), CRB98, 32-33 (bkgrnd), Dawn Hudson,
14 (gaming icon), 18-19 (bkgrnd), Dennis Cox, 34 (left), FotoJagodka, 26 (dog), greatpapa,
27 (bottom), gudron, 4-5 (bkgrnd), 14-15 (bkgrnd), Ilya Akinshin, 40 (bottom), JM – Design,
back cover, 6-7 (bkgrnd), 16-17 (bkgrnd), 26-27 (bkgrnd), Kellie L. Folkerts, 34-35 (stars
bkgrnd), kentoh, 20-21 (bkgrnd), 22-23 (bkgrnd), 24-25 (bkgrnd), Kokhanchikov, 24 (green
apples), Kots, 8-9 (silver, gold medals), Maria Bell, 14 (pizza), Mark R, 30-31 (bkgrnd), Markus
Gann, 20 (bottom), mheld, 16, More Similar Images, 15 (bottom), Pakhnyushcha, 45 (left),
Pennyimages, 24 (red apple), Peter Holecka, 38-39 (bkgrnd), Sebastian Kaulitzki, 8 (bottom),
Sergi Kozhadub, 30 (bottom), sgame, 13 (tetris pieces), Stephen Finn, 34-35 (bkgrnd);
Wikipedia, 13 (top), 26 (Chase the Chuck Wagon game), 34 (middle right)

TABLE OF CONTENTS

Adventure Awaits!

Do you want to fly an F-22 fighter plane? Or play guitar like a rock star? Or cast magic spells to make yourself invisible? Maybe you can't do these things in real life. But you can experience these wonders and more with the click of a button.

Video games entertain and educate. Physical education teachers use *Dance Dance Revolution* to teach fitness. Some people learn about history by playing *Medal of Honor*.

In 2006, Americans spent $7.4 billion on video games. It's safe to say that video games are part of our daily lives.

SELECT   START

Stay Cool!!

Dance Dance Revolution mat.

4

LIVING THE FANTASY

Many video games give people the chance to live out their fantasies. *Guitar Hero* lets players pretend to be rock stars.

Released in the United States in 2005, the game became an instant hit. Players loved to rock out on the guitar-shaped device that controls the game. In time, players could try more instruments, including bass guitar and drums, using different devices in games like *Rock Band*.

Many rock stars loved the game as well. Slash and members of KISS promoted the game.

Guitar Hero guitar

Rock Band guitar

How did video games become so popular? To better understand the importance of video games, we can look to the past. The history of video games is a great adventure story that goes back 50 years.

The story begins with a big idea and a big computer. It starts with a man who dreamed about outer space.

In the Beginning

The First Video Game

Imagine a computer as big as your entire bedroom. The first computers were that large! It took 15 tons (13.6 metric tons) of air conditioning equipment to cool down just one computer.

In the 1960s, college student Steve Russell loved to hack. At that time, a "hack" was a change in computer hardware that opened up new functions.

Russell liked science fiction stories about life future or on other planets. He also enjoyed working the campus computer. Dared by classmates, he started ing a computer game. Almost a year later, in 1962, the deo game was born. Russell called it *Spacewar*.

FACT:

In 1961, a computer sold for more than $100,000. Only a few research universities were able to afford one. In comparison, the average house in 1961 cost $12,500. A person could buy about eight houses for the price of one computer!

The game featured rocket ships sailing across a green screen. They fired torpedoes at one another while they avoided flying into the sun. The game wowed computer scientists, but few others saw it.

HOW DID IT WORK?

Images created by the earliest computers and TVs were powered by cathode ray technology. A cathode is an electron gun at the end of a funnel-shaped glass tube.

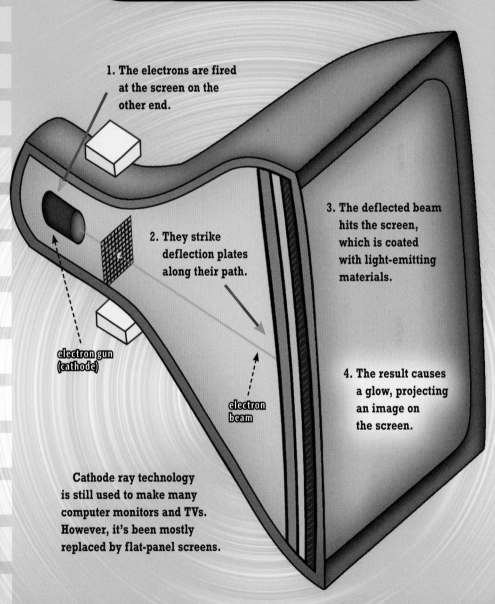

1. The electrons are fired at the screen on the other end.

2. They strike deflection plates along their path.

3. The deflected beam hits the screen, which is coated with light-emitting materials.

4. The result causes a glow, projecting an image on the screen.

electron gun (cathode)

electron beam

Cathode ray technology is still used to make many computer monitors and TVs. However, it's been mostly replaced by flat-panel screens.

cathode—an electron gun that fires electrons at a screen to create an image

electron—a tiny particle that moves around the nucleus of an atom and carries a negative electrical charge

Arcade Fever!

Coin-operated games have been around since the saloon days of the Wild West in the late 1800s. The first ones were gambling devices designed to lure people into the saloon to spend their money.

Most early arcades also included novelties, such as shooting games and jukeboxes that played popular songs. Companies such as Sega made many novelties.

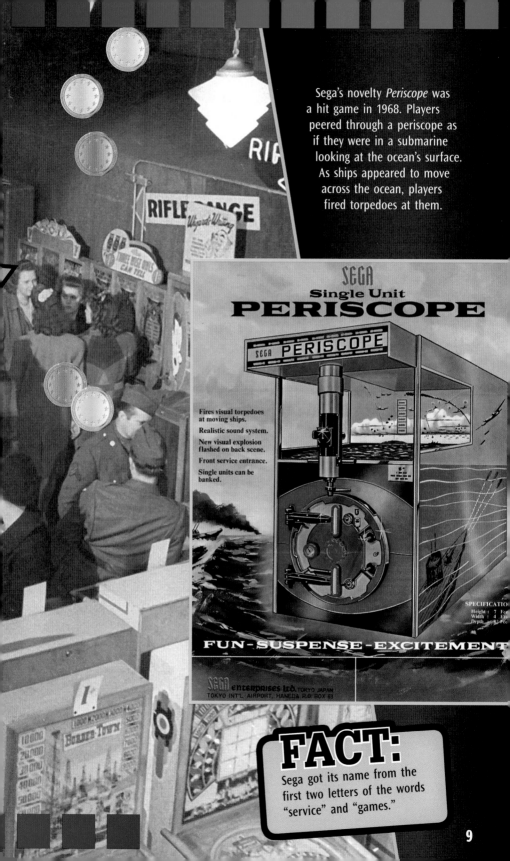

Sega's novelty *Periscope* was a hit game in 1968. Players peered through a periscope as if they were in a submarine looking at the ocean's surface. As ships appeared to move across the ocean, players fired torpedoes at them.

RIFLE RANGE

SEGA
Single Unit
PERISCOPE

SEGA PERISCOPE

Fires visual torpedoes at moving ships.

Realistic sound system.

New visual explosion flashed on back scene.

Front service entrance.

Single units can be banked.

SPECIFICATIO
Height : 7 Fee
Width : 4 Fe
Depth : 5 Fee

FUN-SUSPENSE-EXCITEMENT

SEGA enterprises Ltd. TOKYO JAPAN
TOKYO INT'L AIRPORT, HANEDA P.O. BOX 63

FACT:
Sega got its name from the first two letters of the words "service" and "games."

A Grand Idea

A few years after *Periscope* invaded arcades, engineer Ralph Baer helped change the gaming world. He invented a machine that brought video games to people's homes.

Baer had come to the United States from Germany. He then earned a degree in television engineering.

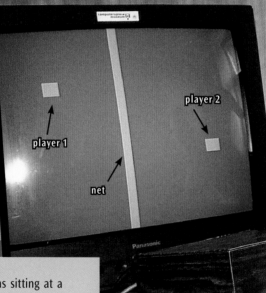

player 2

player 1

net

Panasonic

One day Baer was sitting at a bus stop when an idea struck him. He wondered if there was a way that TV could be made **interactive**. Could it be possible to create a low-cost machine that allowed games to be played on a TV?

interactive—allowing two-way electronic communication, as between a person and a television or computer

GAMES PEOPLE PLAY

The Odyssey offered players a variety of games. Among them were:

* Tennis   * Roulette
* Hockey   * Haunted House
* Simon Says   * Cat and Mouse
* Football

Baer was a manager at a military equipment company. He put his best engineers to work on the idea. Nearly six years later, in 1972, the first Magnavox Odyssey shipped to dealers. It cost $100 and only played a few simple games, such as *Tennis*. But soon Americans were scrambling to own these machines.

FACT: Ralph Baer is known as the father of video games.

Ralph Baer plays *Tennis* on the Magnavox Odyssey.

Early Games That Rocked the World

Through the years, many video games have been created. A few of them, however, have really made history. They amazed and amused millions of players who first tried them in arcades. Some of these games remain popular even though they've been around a very long time.

Space Invaders

People flocked to arcades to play *Space Invaders* when it was released in 1978.

In the game, players move a small cannon at the bottom of the screen.

FACT:
In Japan, *Space Invaders* was so popular that it caused a national coin shortage!

Advancing rows of aliens descend from the top. Players try to shoot all the aliens before the aliens reach the bottom. The game's nonstop action proved irresistible.

Asteroids

Asteroids is similar to Steve Russell's *Spacewar*. Players control a small spaceship as giant asteroids fly all around it. Players can turn the spaceship and use thrusters to escape the asteroids. Blasts from the spaceship's lasers cause the asteroids to break into smaller and faster moving pieces. UFOs add to the mayhem. The UFOs shoot missiles, which the player must avoid.

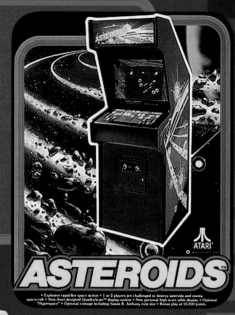

Tetris

Tetris is a simple but addictive game that was created by Soviet scientist Alexey Pajitnov.

It's a puzzle game that features falling pieces that players have to arrange along the bottom of the screen.

Tetris is among the most popular video games of all time.

More than 125 million *Tetris* products have been sold.

NIntendo's *Tetris Attack*

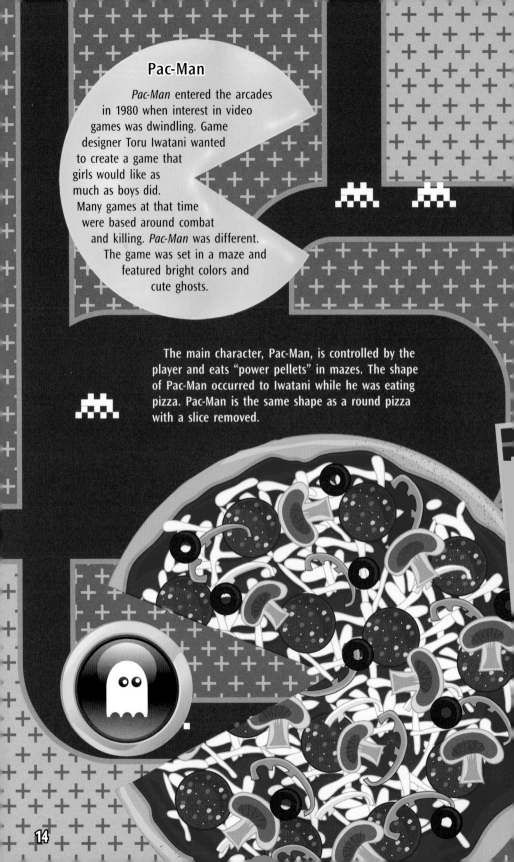

Pac-Man

Pac-Man entered the arcades in 1980 when interest in video games was dwindling. Game designer Toru Iwatani wanted to create a game that girls would like as much as boys did. Many games at that time were based around combat and killing. *Pac-Man* was different. The game was set in a maze and featured bright colors and cute ghosts.

The main character, Pac-Man, is controlled by the player and eats "power pellets" in mazes. The shape of Pac-Man occurred to Iwatani while he was eating pizza. Pac-Man is the same shape as a round pizza with a slice removed.

Because of *Pac-Man*, maze games became more popular than shooting games. A few years later when *Ms. Pac-Man* was released, more than 115,000 units were sold. No video game had ever sold more.

Donkey Kong

Donkey Kong marked the first appearance of Mario. In *Donkey Kong*, Mario is known as Jumpman. He's a carpenter who scales a series of platforms. However, it's not as easy as it sounds. As he climbs the platforms, he also has to leap over barrels tossed by a giant ape. Jumpman's goal is to reach the platforms' tops and rescue a princess.

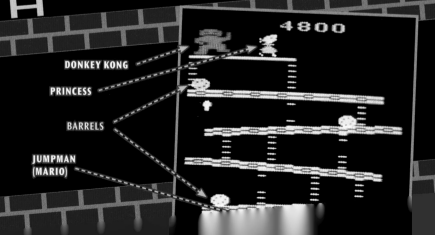

DONKEY KONG

PRINCESS

BARRELS

JUMPMAN (MARIO)

4800

Chapter 2

Home Invasion

Atari
Hits the
Scene

In the 1960s, Nolan Bushnell was a student at the University of Utah. It was one of a few places in the world that had computers at that time. Bushnell learned programming and early computer languages. He even invented his own games.

Bushnell was awed by Steven Russell's *Spacewar* game. Bushnell decided to build a home version of the game. The result was *Computer Space*. His coin-operated machine, built by Nutting Associates, came out in 1971. It promptly flopped.

But Bushnell was determined. He talked his friend Ted Dabney into investing $250 to start their own company. They named their company Atari. In time that $250 investment would be worth millions.

PONG

One of Bushnell's best finds was engineer Al Alcorn. Nolan asked Alcorn to design an electronic ping-pong game. Alcorn surprised Bushnell by adding sound effects and other improvements. The result was called *Pong*. The game swept into arcades across the United States. The *Pong* craze launched Atari as a serious company.

FACT: The word Atari comes from the Japanese board game *Go*. It means "check."

In 1975, Atari entered the home **console** market. It made a home *Pong* system to compete with the Magnavox Odyssey. Most retailers considered the product a passing fad. However, Sears agreed to sell the home *Pong* system. All 150,000 systems were sold in a single season.

In 1976, Fairchild Camera and Instrument released the Channel F. The Channel F was the first home console system that had interchangeable cartridges it called videocarts.

POWER ON COLOR OFF B•W TV TYPE VIDEO COMPUTER SYSTEM™ GAME SELECT GAME RESET

ATARI 2600
POLE POSITION™

ATARI®

In 1977, the Atari VCS hit the market. It was one of the first cartridge systems. Each of the system's nine cartridges offered a different game.

The console also came with a unique pair of "joysticks" that set it apart from the competition. About 400,000 systems were ordered by retailers. Over time, the system became very popular.

A joystick works as a control for a player. Depending on the game being played, it can allow a player to move up or down, left or right. Buttons on joysticks also allow players to fire in shooting games.

Consoles such as the Atari VCS are called hardware. The games are the software. The first hardware systems released came with the games hardwired into them. Once you bought the system, you could only play the few games it offered.

Other companies soon realized that offering cartridges was the way of the future. They started making their own videocarts. By purchasing cartridges, there were no limits to the games people could play with the same console.

Plan B

Meanwhile, back at Atari, Nolan Bushnell left the company he founded. But he had another idea—and it still involved games.

Bushnell started Chuck E. Cheese, a pizza arcade. Along with mechanical animal shows, the restaurant included plenty of exciting video games.

Nolan Bushnell became a multi-millionaire all over again after founding Chuck E. Cheese.

PIZZA TIME T

The Art of a Good Game

Designers put a lot of thought into how games look. Maybe the artwork is beautiful. Perhaps it's complex. Or maybe it's just plain goofy or fun.

Dragon's Lair

Arcades depended on games that offered something new and exciting to keep customers coming in. In 1983 Cinematronics released *Dragon's Lair*. This game pioneered the use of laser disc technology.

The game was drawn by Disney **animator** Don Bluth. The comical graphics of *Dragon's Lair* wowed players.

Players assumed the role of the witless knight Dirk. They guided Dirk through a castle filled with poisons and dragons.

animator—an artist who creates images that appear to move

Q*bert

As technology advanced, so did a programmer's ability to make games that looked like art.

At Gottlieb and Company, artist Jeff Lee was inspired by the artwork of M.C. Escher. Lee used his inspiration to create a pyramid-like stack of 3-D cubes.

The hero of Lee's game had no arms or legs. However, the hero could shoot his enemies with his hoselike nose.

Originally the game was called *Snots and Boogers*. Eventually, with the help of other designers, a new hero emerged. Q*bert, who had legs, saved other characters rather than shooting snot. He tried to outwit enemies, such as Coily the bouncing snake. *Q*bert* used both comedy and strategy to keep gamers interested.

FACT: Q*bert was so popular that he became a Saturday morning cartoon.

The game's goal is to have Q*bert jump from cube to cube to change the cubes' colors. Each round ends when all the cubes are the desired color.

Green creatures can't hurt Q*bert, but they can cause him problems. After Q*bert has changed a cube's color, a green creature might change it back.

Coily tries to jump on Q*bert and kill him.

Hopping on a green ball freezes all the characters except for Q*bert.

!#?

21

Early Designers and "Easter Eggs"

Many early software designers were not allowed to take credit for the games they made. A designer might spend three or four months working on a game. They created programs that made games work. They chose the art. They even picked the music. Yet their names were not even on the video games' packages.

game program™
ADVENTURE
Use with Joystick Controllers

ATARI®
CX2613

Label, Program & Audiovisual © 1978 ATARI, INC.

Atari designer Warren Robinett grew tired of being overlooked. While working on the game *Adventure*, he created a secret room. A secret room in a video game is called an Easter Egg. ■

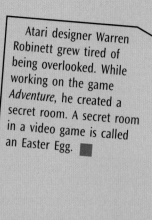

...Created by... Warren Robinett

Players could only find Robinett's Easter Egg after picking up a tiny dot. They used the dot to pass through the wall into the room. When a player got inside the room, the screen flashed the words "Created by Warren Robinett."

Robinett's Easter Egg wasn't discovered until a year after the game was released. People loved the idea!

Many designers started creating games that had hidden wonders that only the most dedicated players could discover.

Giving credit to game designers is still an issue today. Sometimes designers are recognized, but often they are not.

The dragon from Atari's *Adventure*

A Computer in Every Home?

In the late 1970s, **chip** technology became affordable enough for manufacturers to make the first home computers. Video games again led the way home by showing that computers could be "friendly" entertainment centers.

Steve Jobs

Steve Wozniak

The first computer engineers built computers in their garages. Among them were friends Steve Jobs and Steve Wozniak.

In 1976, they founded Apple Computers in a garage workshop. Just four years later, Apple Computers was a billion-dollar company.

chip—a tiny piece of silicon with electronic circuits printed on it that is used in a computer

In 1977, Commodore launched its first PET home computer. It would be followed by the Commodore 64. The Commodore 64 was one of the most popular computers ever. Home computers could be used in home offices or as educational tools. And they could also be used to play games!

C: commodore   **PET** 2001 Series   personal computer

Many early computer games were text-based. Games such as *Colossal Cave Adventure* opened up huge, interactive worlds. Players moved characters by typing commands such as "go north" or "pick up key" on the computer keyboard.

A Passing Fad?

The End of Games?

In 1981, making video games was a $5 billion industry. There were about 24,000 arcades and 1.5 million video game machines in operation throughout the world.

Video games seemed to be everywhere. And everyone wanted to be involved with them.

Purina released *Chase the Chuck Wagon*. It was a game based on a dog food commercial.

Chase the Chuck Wagon had dogs going through a maze to find a horse drawn covered wagon.

Sorry We're CLOSED

So many companies made games that the market became full of poor products. Prices fell, driving companies such as Mattel and ColecoVision out of business.

The ultimate loser was the video game player, who quickly lost interest. More than 2,000 arcades closed in 1983.

Atari also struggled. It rushed games into production, and some of them flopped. One big mistake was the game *E.T.* It's considered among the worst games ever made. Atari hurried production of the game to get it in stores for the Christmas shopping season. Critics could tell. They criticized the plot and gameplay. They also complained about the way the game looked.

So many bad games were produced that Atari ended up dumping millions of cartridges into a New Mexico landfill. Bulldozers crushed the unwanted games! Newspapers wrote headlines proclaiming "The End of Games." Video games were dismissed as just one more passing fad.

27

Nintendo Fills the Void

Nintendo was a 100-year-old Japanese company that first made playing cards before it began making video games. Its first gaming system, called Famicom, was released in Japan in 1983. Two years later, it released the system in the United States under the name Nintendo Entertainment System (NES). It arrived at a time when few people wanted anything to do with video games anymore.

Nintendo wanted to show that the NES was more than just a gaming machine. The first NES came with a light gun. It also had a small robot that sold separately. The system became popular almost instantly. Video games began to make a comeback. People went crazy for games such as *Super Mario Bros.*, *Metroid*, and *The Legend of Zelda*. By 1987, Nintendo controlled most of the gaming market.

1. First came the Nintendo Entertainment System,

FACT: Nintendo means "leave luck to heaven" in Japanese.

3. Nintendo 64 was released in 1996.

2. Then came Super Nintendo in the early 1990s,

NINTENDO64

Nintendo succeeded by creating fun games that people of all ages loved to play. Players also enjoyed the games' characters. Each seemed to have his or her own amusing personality.

Sometimes characters from one Nintendo game would show up in another game. When *Mike Tyson Punch Out* came out in 1987, Donkey Kong was in the audience cheering!

In *Mike Tyson Punch Out*, players control Little Mac, a boxer making his way up the ranks. This character fights a series of fictional boxers until he gets to the championship round. Then Little Mac battles Mike Tyson. At the time the game came out, Tyson was the World Heavyweight champion.

In the Palm of Your Hand

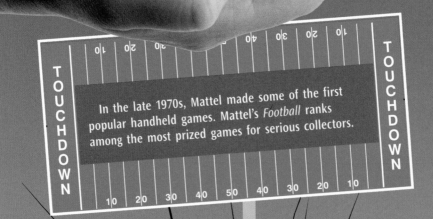

In the late 1970s, Mattel made some of the first popular handheld games. Mattel's *Football* ranks among the most prized games for serious collectors.

Fellow toymaker Milton Bradley also gave the handheld business a shot. The company released the Microvision in 1979. It was the first handheld system to use interchangeable cartridges. Unfortunately, both the cartridges and the system's screen were easily broken.

FACT: The first handheld systems used the same LED technology that makes some watches light up.

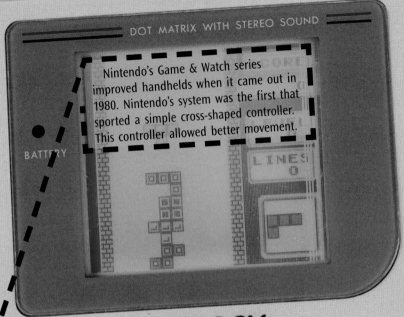

DOT MATRIX WITH STEREO SOUND

Nintendo's Game & Watch series improved handhelds when it came out in 1980. Nintendo's system was the first that sported a simple cross-shaped controller. This controller allowed better movement.

BATTERY

LINES
0

Nintendo **GAME BOY**™

But no other system has matched what Nintendo did with the Game Boy in 1989. More than 35 million units were sold, thanks to the inclusion of *Tetris*. Game Boy became the most popular handheld system of all time.

Other systems, such as the 2004 PlayStation Portable, have challenged the Game Boy. However, none have come close to dethroning the champion of handhelds.

B

A

SELECT

START

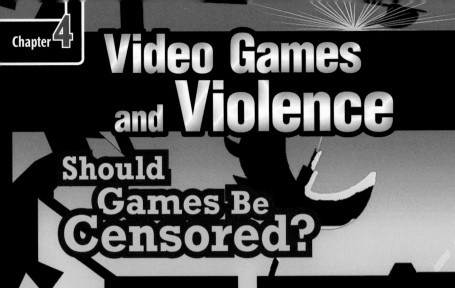

Chapter 4

Video Games and Violence

Should Games Be Censored?

Controversies about video games are as old as the games themselves.

In 1976, Exidy Games released a driving game called *Death Race*. In the game, players run over creatures the company called gremlins. When a gremlin is smashed by a car, the creature screams. Then a little white cross rises up in place of the body. Because its original title was *Pedestrian*, the game's horrifying intent was hard to deny. Many believed the gremlins really represented people.

In the early 1990s, game makers continued pushing boundaries.

Midway's *Mortal Kombat* included blood spatters and grisly kills.

In the year 2000 hit and run driving is no longer a crime. It's the NATIONAL SPORT!

DAVID CARRADINE

DEATH RACE 2000

DAVID CARRADINE IN "DEATH RACE 2000" STARRING SIMONE GRIFFETH AND SYLVESTER STALLONE
ORIGINAL STORY BY PRODUCED BY DIRECTED BY RELEASED BY
SCREENPLAY BY
ROBERT THOM AND CHARLES B. GRIFFITH · IB MELCHIOR · ROGER CORMAN · PAUL BARTEL · focus film distributors

The 1975 movie version of *Death Race* had people in place of the game's gremlins.

Sega

Nintendo

TAKING THE HIGH ROAD

While Sega claimed to aim its games at adults, Nintendo prided itself on being a family system.

To protect its reputation, Nintendo heavily censored all the games made for its systems. Even religious symbols such as crosses were banned from games such as *Castlevania*. Designers often were upset by the censorship. However, they had to follow Nintendo's rules in order to work there.

Congress
Gets Involved

In 1993, Congress held hearings to debate violence in games. Experts from many fields issued warnings about the dangers of games to youth.

NON-STOP ACTION!

NIGHT TRAP

OVER 1½ HOURS OF REAL VIDEO

SEGA

SEGA CD

In *Night Trap*, players tried to protect a group of college-age girls from vampires. Critics of the game said it was too violent. They also objected to the way the girls were dressed.

Congress held a second set of hearings in 1994. Sega responded to the hearings by developing its own rating system.

Another result of the hearings was increased public awareness of violent video games. One violent game targeted by Congress was *Night Trap*, which became a bestseller.

DO VIOLENT GAMES MAKE VIOLENT KIDS?

In 1994, the Entertainment Software Rating Board (ESRB) formed. The ESRB designed ratings to help protect children from inappropriate games. Still, the issue of violence in games has not gone away.

Studies about the effect of violence in video games have not reached any real conclusions. They neither prove nor disprove any connection between video games and youth violence. In fact, the violence rate among youth has been dropping steadily since 1994.

OK TO PLAY?

CHECK THE RATINGS *ON EVERY* VIDEO GAME BOX.

To take full advantage of the ESRB Rating System, it is important for parents and other customers to check the Rating Symbol suggesting age appropriateness on the front of the game package, and the content descriptor on the back of the package. Content descriptors indicate elements in a game that may have triggered a particular rating and may be of interest or concern.

ON FRONT OF GAME PACKAGING

	Early Childhood	May be suitable for ages 3 and older. Contains no material that parents would find inappropriate.
	Everyone	May be suitable for ages 6 and older. Titles in this category may contain minimal cartoon, fantasy or mild violence and/or use of mild language.
	Everyone 10+	May be suitable for ages 10 and older. Titles in this category may contain more cartoon, fantasy or mild violence, mild language, and/or minimal suggestive themes.
	Teen	May be suitable for ages 13 and older. Titles in this category may contain violence, suggestive themes, crude humor, minimal blood, simulated gambling, and/or infrequent use of strong language.
	Mature	May be suitable for ages 17 and older. Titles in this category may contain intense violence, blood and gore, sexual content, and/or strong language.
A⦾	**Adults Only**	Should only be played by persons 18 years and older. Titles in this category may include prolonged scenes of intense violence and/or graphic sexual content and nudity.

ON BACK OF GAME PACKAGING

Content descriptors are found on the back of the box. Go to www.ESRB.org for a complete listing of content descriptors.

www.ESRB.org

A *Doom* game CD

ESRB ratings help children and parents decide which games are appropriate.

FACT:
In 1999, Dylan Klebold and Eric Harris killed 13 students, including themselves, at Columbine High School in Colorado. The killers were fans of the violent video game *Doom*. They spoke of the game on tapes they recorded before the shootings. Some people believe the video game played a part in the boys' choice to use violence.

Chapter 5

The Competition Heats Up

The Next Generation

By the time Sega released the Genesis in 1989, Nintendo already dominated the industry. However, Sega benefited by being one of the first 16-bit gaming machines on the market. Because others were only 8 bits, Sega's new system offered more exciting graphics. Sega also advertised—a lot! If Nintendo had high kid appeal, then Sega targeted young adults. Sega's ads featured the famous "Sega Scream."

Designers were eager to make games for the Genesis. Games produced for the system were almost as good as arcade versions. Companies such as Electronic Arts marketed great sports games for the Genesis, including *John Madden Football*.

Enter Sonic the Hedgehog. Lightning-quick and hyperactive, Sonic leapt across a colorful landscape. He jumped over chasms, grabbed coins, and spun upside down through loops on his way to instant popularity. Sega had its flagship character.

Sega

Nintendo

In its battle with Nintendo, Sega proved that it could go toe-to-toe. By the end of 1992, Sega controlled 55 percent of the gaming market.

21   33

8-bit tennis game

The image on an 8-bit machine is very limited when compared to the image on a 32-bit machine. The 8-bit machine's tennis game looks old-fashioned next to the exciting graphics of a newer game.

Düsseldorf Open

32-bit tennis game

A BIT ABOUT BITS

A bit is the building block of computer memory. The number of bits matters greatly when it comes to graphics. A one-bit image is monochrome. An eight-bit image supports 256 colors. A 32-bit image supports true colors, like those you see in real life. So the number of bits in a gaming machine indicates how realistic the colors and images will appear.

Sonic Boom

Originally, Sony tried teaming with Nintendo to make a compact disc (CD) player for its gaming system. Game machines using CDs dominated the 1990s. With the exception of the Nintendo 64, most companies converted to this format. CDs can store a large amount of information. They also are cheap to produce.

But Nintendo didn't want to team with Sony. Spurned by Nintendo, Sony built a system of its own.

Sony's PlayStation debuted in the United States in 1995. The system offered awesome 3-D graphics. The built-in CD-drive allowed full motion video. More than 100 companies signed on to make games for the system before its launch.

The public also loved PlayStation. About 100 million units were sold!

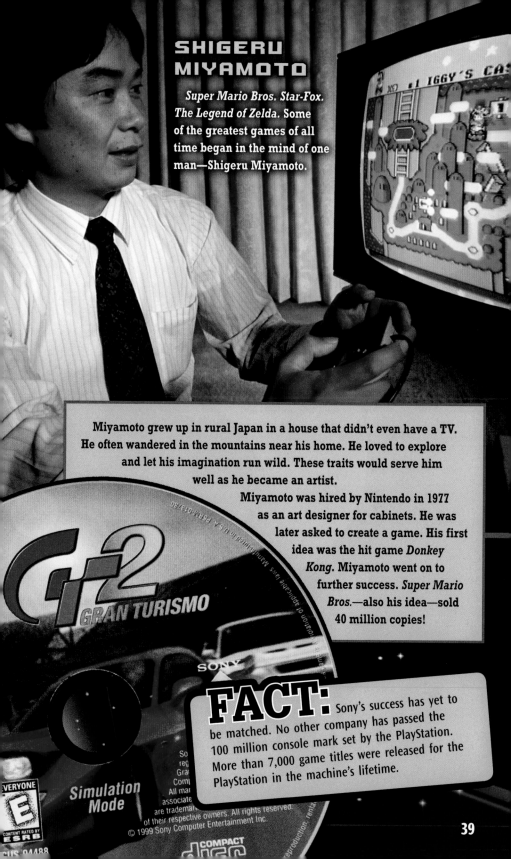

SHIGERU MIYAMOTO

Super Mario Bros. Star-Fox. The Legend of Zelda. Some of the greatest games of all time began in the mind of one man—Shigeru Miyamoto.

Miyamoto grew up in rural Japan in a house that didn't even have a TV. He often wandered in the mountains near his home. He loved to explore and let his imagination run wild. These traits would serve him well as he became an artist.

Miyamoto was hired by Nintendo in 1977 as an art designer for cabinets. He was later asked to create a game. His first idea was the hit game *Donkey Kong*. Miyamoto went on to further success. *Super Mario Bros.*—also his idea—sold 40 million copies!

FACT:

Sony's success has yet to be matched. No other company has passed the 100 million console mark set by the PlayStation. More than 7,000 game titles were released for the PlayStation in the machine's lifetime.

39

Chapter 6

Looking Toward the Future

The Internet and Beyond

Broderbund stunned gamers in 1993 with *Myst*. The game's beautiful 3-D scenes, haunting music, and challenging puzzles immersed gamers in a new world. *Myst* sold 12 million copies.

Also in 1993, ID Software released *Doom*. With this new game, the era of first-person shooters dawned. Players felt like they were shooting instead of making characters shoot. Heavy metal music and intense action provided an experience that felt so real that many players dreamed about *Doom* at night.

By the late 1990s, the Internet was changing the world. Online gaming and social networking took off. Massively Multiplayer Online Role Playing Games, or MMORPGs, appeared. One of these games, *Neverwinter Nights*, let a player assume a virtual identity and team up with others around the world for gaming adventures.

MMORPGs can include hundreds, thousands, or even millions of players. The themes of the games are as varied as the people who play them. Some MMORPGs include:

* *City of Heroes*   * *Toontown*

* *Darkfall*   * *City of Villains*

* *ROBLOX*   * *Wizard 101*

FACT: By 2008, another online game, *World of Warcraft*, had more than 11 million subscribers.

Getting Active With Wii

Near the end of 2006, a new console started getting people off their couches and into the action.

With a variety of games and fitness programs, the Wii appealed to people of all ages.

The Nintendo Wii uses a remote control to sense a player's movements.

It became so popular, stores across the globe couldn't get them in fast enough to keep up with demand.

It's as if the player is really playing baseball, bowling, or golfing.

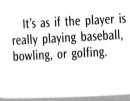

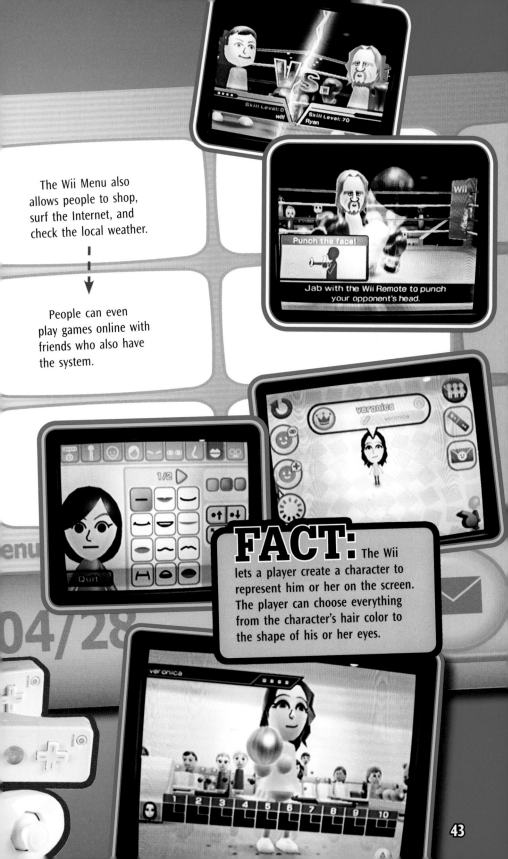

The Wii Menu also allows people to shop, surf the Internet, and check the local weather.

People can even play games online with friends who also have the system.

FACT: The Wii lets a player create a character to represent him or her on the screen. The player can choose everything from the character's hair color to the shape of his or her eyes.

X Marks the Spot

Microsoft already had a billion-dollar empire before Bill Gates excited the gaming world. He announced that Microsoft planned to begin producing a gaming console in 2000. The system officially launched in November 2001.

Bill Gates unveiled the Xbox system, which set off a worldwide frenzy.

The public loved it. Microsoft had established itself as an important player in the video game business.

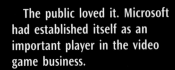

But the Xbox faced tough competition when PlayStation 3 was released in 2006. This system uses new Blu-ray technology and includes free interactive gaming over the Internet. Xbox 360 also allows interactive gaming, but users pay extra.

The Nintendo Wii, Xbox 360, and PlayStation 3 compete for your dollars. In order to stay ahead of the competition, these companies will continue to improve gaming technology.

The Xbox 360 features a wireless controller. You can be up to 30 feet (9 meters) away from the game and still be able to play.

AN UNEXPECTED TREASURE

In the mid-1980s, when Tanner Sandlin was about 11, he bought the video game *Air Raid*. He paid between $5 and $10 for it. At the time, he was disappointed with his purchase. Once he started playing it, he didn't think it was much fun. In fact, he often traded the game with friends for other games. But *Air Raid* kept coming back to him.

It turns out that Sandlin was really lucky. Few copies of *Air Raid* exist now. Because Sandlin even kept the game's box, his was the only known complete copy in the world. In April 2010, Sandlin was rewarded for the care he took of *Air Raid*. He sold it on eBay for $31,600!

From *Spacewar* to *World of Warcraft*, games have undergone many exciting developments. The games of tomorrow may be the games you create!

GLOSSARY

animator (AH-ni-may-tur)—an artist who creates images that appear to move

bit (BIT)—binary digit; the building block of computer memory

cathode (KATH-ohd)—an electron gun that fires electrons at a screen to create an image

chip (CHIP)—a tiny piece of silicon with electronic circuits printed on it that is used in a computer

console (KON-sohl)—a device that includes the hardware needed to play video games

electron (i-LEC-trahn)—a tiny particle that moves around the nucleus of an atom and carries a negative electrical charge

hardware (HARD-wayr)—the main console that houses the gaming machine or computer

interactive (int-ur-AK-tiv)—allowing two-way electronic communication, as between a person and a television or computer

monochrome (MAHN-oh-crohm)—one color, or different shades of one color

science fiction (SIE-enss FIC-shun)—stories about life in the future or on other planets

software (SOFT-wayr)—interchangeable units, such as cartridges, floppy discs, and CDs that store video games

READ MORE

Andersen, Neil. *At the Controls: Questioning Video and Computer Games.* Media Literacy. Mankato, Minn.: Capstone Press, 2007.

Berens, Kate and Geoff Howard. *The Rough Guide to Video Games.* Rough Guides. New York: The Penguin Group, 2008.

Frederick, Shane. *Gamers Unite!: The Video Game Revolution.* Pop Culture Revolution. Minneapolis: Compass Point Books, 2010.

Thompson, Lisa. *Game On: Have You Got What It Takes to be a Video Game Developer?* On the Job. Minneapolis: Compass Point Books, 2010.

INTERNET SITES

FactHound offers a safe, fun way to find Internet sites related to this book. All of the sites on FactHound have been researched by our staff.

Here's all you do:

Visit *www.facthound.com*

Type in this code: **9781429647922**